Intert

Special thanks to the people that's helped me on this path of discover, along with my family and my amazing fiancé Andrea.

The moon is in reach, why stop their...shoot for the stars!

Intertwining Souls

TWO IS BETTER THAN ONE

Our soul's intertwining as one

With different heart beats

That is not in sync

One is overloading with duties

Till the other one is extinct

But the dearly try to beat a rhythm of the same drum.

As time goes by

The pulses subside

A miraculous occurrence happens

The loving souls are reconnecting

They wisely listen to one another synchronizing

Joining the same beat of their own drum

(Because two is better than one)

Rocky Bradford

Intertwining Souls

ONLY 4 LETTERS

its only 4 letters,

but simply as it is

it's too hard to say,

once you've said it

you have removed your veil of your heart

to the painful riches of life;

it's not preserved in a perfect state,

but founded in sweet and sours of reality,

it is an invisible force that connects,

broken parts of life;

and we as human beings

search for the affection of emotion,

Its only 4 letters,

we ask for it,

we kill because of it,

we need for it,

we get sad because of it,

we crave its passion,

the warmth of affection,

but we are scared of it,

what it might open,

what it might bring,

bringing happiness,

therefore, making you hurt,

yet, desire it, in which,

Intertwining Souls

at the same time, we fear it..

its only 4 letters

4 strong deep letters,

together as the word forms,

becomes immortal,

an efficient energy we strive to possess,

but, we cannot contain the magnificent essence of love.

But how?

Why not?

Its only 4 letters,

L.O.V.E.

Rocky Bradford

Intertwining Souls

Cocoon

Dying within, either way trapped I am.
By the thick layers of skin,
the anxious feeling of creepy crawlers crawling on my neck.
Waiting for the day,
that ONE date,
causing rupture to the cocoon.
Sweet smells of oxygen seeping thru the cracks.
My pores of Hyde, flaring for truth
the restless winds slithering down my spine,
clicking of bones rejuvenating my heart
turning vibrations into thumping,
awakening the sleeping beauty,
becoming alive,
remembering the past,
wondering of the present,
forward looking for what shall become.
Mind-boggling,
I draw myself back in
(inhaling & Exhaling)
before I embark on this journey.
Courageous I am! With opportunities of hope
In control now!
I explode out of my hollow emptiness,
my colorful wings flapping, hovering over my old self.
Accepting my transformed vessel,
gathering the earthly dusts swarming around me,
Finally taking off!!! Soaring towards the horizon
beginning the new start of what shall be my new destiny!

Rocky Bradford

Intertwining Souls

Am I worth It?

Am I worth it?
Having this precious air inside my lungs?
To cash in that bullet inside my gun...
Am I worth it?
For someone to love me for who i am,
to find comfort for things I don't understand.
Am I worth it?
Having a merciful god,
sending his son to die for my sins?!
Am I worth it?
To have lived after so many O.Ds
due to the needle inside my skin!
Am I worth it?
People to care and cry about me,
to be a man, husband and a dad.
Am I worth it?
Having a full stomach,
while having clothes on my back.
Am I worth it?
Having a mother and a father still married,
having an education plus being athletic.
Am I worth it?
For someone to spend the rest of their life with me,
am I worth it?
For people to think about or consider,
am I worth it?
I ask myself again! Am I worth it???
I see their beautiful smiles growing up being learners and teachers of their own.

Intertwining Souls

I AM WORTH IT!
To see my kids bloom into flowering angels!
It's all worth it!!!

Rocky Bradford

Intertwining Souls

MY HEART

My hearts struggling in quick-sand,
as the river of life passes thru my arteries,
Tuning into my body sensations,
every muscle in me,
Releasing and contracting.
the gut of my stomach,
overlapping my skull,
holding my breath,
till I'm still,
and no longer in fall,
because my hearts in quick-sand,
every pulsating beat,
keeps it above the sand,
till it is surrenders and is conquered,
my hearts in quick-sand
I have fallen for you,
I'm now floating on romance,
my heart is suffocating in it.

Rocky Bradford

Intertwining Souls
Piece by Piece

Ima be single the rest of my life,
You scarred m carear e till the day I die.
What you did totally affected me,
So now, my soul's incomplete.
My heart is shattered and broken,
I'm picking up the pieces at this exact moment;
Trying to put them together but they just won't stick,
Every women I've kissed,
Isn't the same because they're not your lips.
So now I have this spark inside me like a flame,
Needing to be ignited and set free,
Because in the beginning it was supposed to be you and me!
The lies you said,
The promises un kept,
Leaving my heart broken,
Beating to death!
But that's love at its finest, wouldn't you say?
Taking you back,
So you can just walk away.
Putting me in this funk and pain,
Never ever gonna be able to love again!
But what the future holds...I don't know
Hopefully it's something magical and bright,
My heart piecing itself together,
Pumping to a new life.
That's something to look upon.
So I'm not giving up.
Just starting over,
While I pick up my pieces....

Rocky Bradford

Intertwining Souls

Random

Honestly wish I was dead!
Everything would be easier said
No bills or emotions
I wish I was dead.
I'm jus an angel ready to go home,
This place earth is far too gone.
Why can't life be easy,
I'm willing to lose the fight,
That's jus on a bad day,
The thoughts I want to say,
But I can't leave because your not coming with.
And there's no guarantee ill see u again,
So I confront my demons and fight them off.
Not for me but just for you!
You are a diamond in the ocean
I can't wait till we shine together over the 7 seas!

Rocky Bradford

Intertwining Souls
<u>Circle of Life</u>

Brass of rosewood,

Pollinating fumes of beauty.

Cascading ripples into timeless tears.

Daggering splashes of whirlwinds of enchantment,

Echoing off mahogany seeders,

Transcending melodies from East to West,

Unaccustomed but capricious.

Dancing, carried amount the tunnels of the wind.

Flocks of whispering robins,

Chattering aloud.

Till the second Sun brings nothing but scavengers,

Restarting life as a phoenix,

To the birth of Rah once more!

Rocky Bradford

Intertwining Souls

Wanna Be

I want to be the people I Idolize,
wanting the women, the fame,
everyone knowing my name;
down to the fire flies,
stuck into the big dark sky,
being luminous, shiny and bright,
soaring and shooting,
as you make a wish but,
you look deeper into the distance,
you begin to see a cluster of us
made into a constellation,
just with anything in life,
how hard do you want to be seen?
A pebble or a rock?
Do you want your name engraved into the side walk?
How far are you willing to go?
Having a dim light or one that glows?
So...
Do you want to be a star???

Rocky Bradford

Intertwining Souls
24 hrs.

12 hrs Of light, followed by 12 hrs of night,
I often wonder will you forever be by my side?
12hrs of light, followed by 12 hrs of night,
I stare into space, hoping to soon see ur face,
Sometimes I'm weak in the day, & cry in the night!
12 hrs of light, followed by 12 hrs of night,
the sun will soon come out & dry up all the showers, & this is how my mind wonders in 24 hrs!

Martrice White

Intertwining Souls

27 YEARS LATER

I remember when we met
In 1984 we were set
Friends from then on, without a doubt
Said we would never live without
But time moves on and then we do too
Got caught up in the "cootie" schmooze

We wriggled our noses and turned away
we thought we could go at least a day
But no, instead we played chase all over the playground every day

But time goes on and then we two threw
aside that stage and I was with you

Again we sided it was us two as one
who cares what others thought, we had fun

Many years had passed and I developed a love
each day, each month, each year I thought of you, angels sang from above

Being a foolish child, you drifted away
Until the unthinkable happened 27 years later
I never thought I'd find you 27 years later
That one day we would be together again after 27 years <3

Dedicated to David Street... I'm so happy that I found you. I love you with all my heart and soul. <3

Chelleigh Street

Intertwining Souls
Addiction of a Cig

I was one of many out the pack of 20. Each one of us wondering what our destiny held; contemplating on that spark of life and how our story was going to be told. Would I ever experience this? Or, would I be that one for that person to look upon and reminisce about all the harm my family has done. How would I be used?? During the bathroom? After a meal? After sex? After or before a mind altering drug?? Or, jus due to habit with no purpose at all.

As I stood in that nightly, bottomless pit; I was hoping for the best but expecting the worse. That's when a spiritual hand picked me up while I was still trapped inside my box. It lifted me out of the abyss, appreciating the scenery and fragrances. So far, my life felt complete, therefore, couldn't imagine how my life could get any better. That's when my sights located these dancing spectrums of colors--red, yellow and blue.

As the dancing, luminous spark of life approached, I felt its seductive warmth and I surrendered to it. The feeling was like no other feeling I've ever encountered, it was indescribable, and it was orgasmic!
The sense of pleasure and the effect it had on me at the time, I didn't know until it was too late. The heinous pyro had a different turn of events in store for me. Helplessly, I could slowly begin to feel my body degenerating into ash. As the inedible end came near as the creeping flow of lava render closer and closer. I thought strongly in my cotton filled mind, in which, I was debating against myself--how could I live on?? How can I live forever?? How can I leave a legacy behind??

As the sparking volcanic ash came to swallow me whole, I had a sudden epiphany at the very last puff! I will evermore live on forever as the result of CANCER!

The end

Rocky Bradford

Intertwining Souls

<u>Air</u>

As the last stitch is finished, I begin to have consciousness

Programmed with the idea of just do it

But I can not

My soles are soulless, but I have life

Thread me together

I am stylish while holding my tongue

I walk pass so many competitors, I stand in place observing and watching the potential candidates

But surely, I'll find my soul mate sweeping them off their feet

Perfectly fitting comfortably

They now have me

And I have them

J's on their feet

Rocky Bradford

Intertwining Souls

Amends

When you were just little I was the HERO that taught you how to talk,
when you were just little I was the HERO that taught you how to walk....
I spun you around a few times and
it all came to an end...
Each walking off, no longer a flock... and
Now you all call me "friend"...
I'm sorry for my actions, that was not the message I intended to send,
Rest assured though, I will find a way to make amends
Amen.

Starla Mullins

Intertwining Souls

ANGEL INSIDE OF ME

such a beautiful soul,
Gods amazing creation,
their energy so bright,
its transcendent,
magnificent glow, wings and halo,
immortality, power and wisdom,
beautiful creatures,
that one day we shall become,
soaring thru the pillows of the heavens,
like an eagle being capricious and free,
living life for all eternity,
my souls an angel,
that's locked up inside of me,
it wants to escape,
scrapping along my rib cage,
aching to burst out my chest,
restless and failing to succeed,
mysteriously roaring inside this shell,
anxiously waiting to be unleashed,
my spirit is hungrier than a lion,
that's the soul of my angel,
which is locked up inside of me!

Rocky Bradford

Intertwining Souls

Bending Knee

I've been lookin for that MAN who said that he would always b there for me, that Man who said he was never leaving me, that MAN who said that he would die for me! I've been lookin a whole life time for HE!
Funny thing is I didn't find him where u would think he'd be?!?
I found him when I got down on my knees & cried to THEE! Then realized that he's ALWAYS been with me!
Just took me a minute to know that no one comes before HE!!

Martrice White

Intertwining Souls

Best friends

My best friend Patron thought he was a celebrity with all this fame.
Still best buds through high school till I met Mary Jane.
Engaged to Mary Jane, my true love in this world;
years past, we broke up, because my heart lied between the Boy and the Girl.
The Girl was my stone, boulder and rock
the Boy was my shield, sword and bronze.
The Girls work was honestly hard,
as for the boy?
He had nothing besides the name Ron.
They both had me feinin'!
Especially Ron, until I got sick!
That's when I told Ron to be gone,
and told her to move on ***ch!!!!!

Rocky Bradford

Intertwining Souls

CARVED

Of all the words you told me the worst were "I love you"
Those cut in the deepest and left me the weakest I have ever been
You broke this shell and dropped the biggest bomb to fall
Now when I message you it's basically like talking to a wall
My words fall on deaf ears and you play a pretty Hellen Keller
They say "Man what things do you even have left to tell her?"
I have plenty because they change every day. From "F You" to "I still love you"
My daily routine has turned into a nonstop graveyard shift and I keep digging dirt
I just use it to pile on my already fertilized problems
Read this as my epitaph because I won't be the last to laugh
You walked all over me girl, but you picked me up at the same time
You showed me I could love again, and taught me I could still be broken
My career is just another little distraction
Work the fingers to the bone so your mind don't have to
Keep your body moving because your heart is on bed rest
It's just recovering for the next test
Problem is I am set up to fail
Ever since they started adding math to letters
I bled my last on the ones that I wrote you
You never sent one back but the words never needed written
My snake bit chest will never get rid of this addictive poison
It will swerve through my veins till my brain dies swollen
My bedroom will forever stay a mess and my bed a welcome coffin
So chisel that tombstone and I will keep paying for the privilege
Yeah he can have what I couldn't, but he shouldn't
Maybe in another time...another universe...but for right now...
It's just another brokenhearted verse.
I wouldn't trade it for anything though. Those times that I won't let go
Heart is still yours...your name is still carved in it.

Jesse Roberts

Chariots of Life

The cold brisk winter night

Carrying on with the chilly winds

Leafs ruffling and branches snapping

Underneath the huge broaden stars.

The owls who-ing while wolfs are howling

At the luminous blue moon

All indeed dying with time

But reincarnated by…

Birds singing, doe's first steps

Flowing thru the warmy seeded rays of sunshine

Rocky Bradford

Colder Than

Colder than Ice cubes,
Colder than being in Alaska in the nude,
Colder than dry ice,
colder than the top of a mountains peak,
colder than the depths of outer space,
colder than freezing rain,
colder than ice cream,
colder than the Artic breeze,
more painful than brain freeze,
colder than hyperthermia,
colder than a lifeless body,
colder than the deepest part of the ocean,
Colder than cold itself!
That's the love of your heart!
Colder than...

Rocky Bradford

Intertwining Souls

DUEL

Indulging focus

In mid concentration

Deep screaming thoughts

Hungrier than starvation

So many pieces in play

Infinite amount of outcomes

Which on will you take?

Easy or the hard way

Sacrificing, strategizing, aggressive or passive

The surest one inquired

Will begin and end the brutality of kings

Ones defeated while on reigns and triumphs

All can be avoided by careful choosing and thoughtful concentration.

Rocky Bradford

Intertwining Souls

FACT OF WHY

Her body is simply amazing

Hypnotizing like a cobra

Agile as a cheetah

Beautiful as the starry nights and crest moon

This celestial creature is not human

Nor from this earth

It is else where

From the heavens above

It must be

In order to have such qualities

Of an angel

It has to be!

You are a blessing of Gods workmanship

But he wasn't finished yet

Your voice

That's cuts deep into my flesh

Giving me chills

Making me aroused of the sight of your burgundy skin

The touch is so tempting

Intertwining Souls

As if it was a forbidden fruit

The more I ponder on the dwelling of your shinning soul

These are just mere facts of why...

ILOVEYOU so dearly!!!

Rocky Bradford

Intertwining Souls

"Farewell to my Hell"

Waking up to u every day, needing u to feel well, falling for ur evil, hiding under ur spell.*Hurting my loved ones, caged up in cell, so many times I've said to u, farewell to my hell.*Feeling ur rush, u took away the pain, yet u left me with misery, indulging in all my shame.*I stole and lied to get to u, I hid myself in ur shell, I need to say to u, farewell to my hell.*You took everything from me, yet I loved the way u made me feel, it seemed like a fantasy, but it was all so real.*I can't do this anymore, I'm feeling stronger as u can tell, it's become easier to say, farewell to my hell.*I once thought I was done with u, but u got back into my head, I took one feel of u, next thing I knew I was dead.*Were done it is over, I want nothing u have to sell, I can finally stand up and say, farewell to my hell!

Briana Smith

Intertwining Souls

Ground Level

You took him when I know it was me you wanted,
Now I'll never give you that chance,
No matter how bad I want to,
See I'd of sacrificed myself just to bring him back,
But I will not do for you anymore, Not even for the crack,
I know now that he is free,
And these days the same goes for me,
See death no longer takes over my soul,
And I'll cherish our memories till I grow old,
Always remembered, Never forgotten,
You become my reason why,
I no longer fear starting from the bottom.

Ashlee Sipes

Intertwining Souls

HELPLESS

As I sit I see shadows closing in,
swallowing me whole,
the mass pressure,
forcing unto my body,
till im breathless,;
stranded in the dark,
I am scared in panic,
blinded and helpless,
violent screams of demons,
tempting me in the midst;
inside the bottomless pit,
I wait till my eyes adjust and
I'm still waiting.
I try to speak and talk but,
I'm mute in silence.
I try to run
instead, I can not move,
I'm stuck like a deer in head lights.
Ironically, the darkness is blacker than cancer
and shadier than the color grey;
mind is pacing and racing,
Wondering why
as i approach this far
I am erased, fading away in the essence of the abyss
searching for HOPE!!!!

And still searching......

Rocky Bradford

Intertwining Souls

Her

I knew I won, with you as my biggest catch.
God told me to pick you from all the rest,
because he knew I would love you the very best.
If anything would ever happen to you,
I wouldn't have a clue what I would do!
I would prolly give up all my heavenly things,
my halo and angel wings,
just so I could spend the rest of my life with you for all eternity!

Rocky Bradford

Intertwining Souls

Time, Night, and Day

I feel like a wild animal I wish the moon was full every day I feel the darkness pull me closer and closer to the edge I creep the view from above precarious and steep as I gaze into the souls of the lost my heart is cold like the winter frost my mind has no rest not even in the distant promises of riches and success they say because you're a child of God you are blessed but the dark makes me feel like a demon possessed cry out in the night all by yourself like a dog that starts to yelp drowning in your own sorrows with no one to help in my dreams I fly far away but reality is Hell the vicious game we play at the end of day what is left to say your bones turn to dust and your spirit flies away leaving this earth, time, night and day.

Caleb Patterson

Intertwining Souls

How Do I Let U Go

how do I let u go
how do I gain closer
I need to know

Everything about u filled my heart
ur laugh, ur smile, ur eyes
our life gave me so much happiness
then I was left with nothing but cries

I remember the warmth of ur heart
the way we we're once in love
now the only way to talk to u
Is to ask the Lord above

U meant so much to me
oh how I miss u so
now I have to learn to move on
and how to let u go

What made u feel u cud no longer go on
why was death the way instead of life
we we're supposed to grow old together
u we're going to make me ur wife

I need to tell u I'm sorry
and I'll always love u so much
I wish I could take it all back
oh God how I missed ur touch

See I held all this grief and guilt
It kept so sad and so low

Intertwining Souls

they say I need to be stronger
yet again, how do I let u go

I stress for answers and knowledge
wonderin why u felt it was the answer
It tears me apart
eating at me like cancer

I guess I have to accept it
I guess I'll never know
yet I ask again
how do I let u go

I miss u more than u know
and I know ur looking down on me
ull always remain in my heart
from all this guilt, I need to be free

Until the day we meet again
In my heart ull remain forever so
now I have to move on
I have to let u go!

I wrote this in rehab, it's to my ex that committed suicide in 2010, R. I. P. Seth.....

Briana Smith

Intertwining Souls

Imagine

On the coast

Viewing the sunset

Toes drenched beneath the sand

As the roaring tides

Splash upon the rocks

I'm at peace with myself

The seagulls soaring

Looking for fish swimming

Life is still rumbling

Thru the day, while I marvel at the scenery

As I wonder in trance

Into the enormous organic fire

Before it dies and everything goes SILENCE.

Rocky Bradford

Intertwining Souls

INHALE EXHALE

I can't stop looking at your photo i keep these feelings down low tho

Sigh and swipe right my thoughts keep me up at night

Our time is fleeting

Its you im breathing

Inhale exhale

Can you hear me screaming

I hate to think of you leaving

Walked into you and you into me

Burning from the inside

With you i feel so alive

My life just lost all meaning

Like my heart stopped beating

Inhale exhale

Inhale exhale

Zach Paige

Intertwining Souls

I wrote this while in treatment- Oct, 2015

it's unbearable
to think of the hurt I've caused
the moments I've missed, the time I've lost
how bad I want them to see
there's a culprit to this madness
and it isn't the real me.
it's unforgettable
the anguish, the torment, the dire need
every morning begging God to stop this pain
just put me out of my misery
believe me when I say there has to be
a culprit to this madness, it isn't the real me
it's emotional
to remember the hurt in my children's eyes
the love they have is unconditional
through every unanswered cry
through unkept promises the maybes and we'll sees
there's a culprit to this madness
but it isn't the real me
it's uncomfortable
to realize how close I came to defeat
to admit I'm powerless and it controls me
I'm ready to confront my unresolved pain
past injustices that cause suffering
recovery starts with honesty I believe
there's a culprit to this madness
and it isn't the real me
it's forgivable
I have acknowledged the issue

Intertwining Souls

all these mistakes don't have to continue
today, I can define a boundary
I can be cautious and vigilant
I can find real peace
there's a culprit to this madness
it's not me.
It's my disease.
~Kasey Zorns 2015~

Intertwining Souls

Little Ninja

March 8th in the evening I lost my nephew who died upon impact of hitting a state vehicle with his car this is the poem that I wrote a few moments ago...

My Ninja Nephew
My nephew's eyes have closed forever
His face, his laugh and smile...
Where once he stood before us,
Pictures now take his place.

Gone Too Soon, my little ninja
from here, your place of birth....
Pinch me, wake me from this... Can ya?
I can't believe that you no longer walk this Earth.

Reality of it is, I know it's true
Yet, I still can't believe
my little ninja, filled with so much life
really had to leave.

We all have loved you from your birth
Watched you grow tall and learn...
My ninja nephew, we shall meet again
when my chores are done and it's my time to return.

Until I see you again, I'll be loving and missing you meeps meeps!!!
Love,
Me Auntie (*la)

Starla Mullins

Intertwining Souls

Love of my Knife

Cold bitterness of stainless steel,
Urging for tender flesh once more.
Pain & Sorrows to those with no affliction,
Earning for their warmth,
Piercing their skin,
forcible entering with no permission..
I turn my body, Climaxing,
Gazing upon their eyes,
till their iris is colorless..
Drained of their soul,
Instantly removed,
REPEATEDLY,
hunger for the taste,
once more..
Embracing the think red puddle,
while the air makes me
cold once again...
because I'm lonely,
due to killing my
only friend.....VICTIM

Rocky Bradford

Intertwining Souls

Me Myself & I

My life force feels like it is
being absorbed.
I honestly wish I wasn't even born,
Only death would set me free,
Tie the knot on the noose and...
1... 2..... 3.......
As I fell,
life flashed in front of my eyes,
my loved ones appeared in
thin air and in my sights,
I can't believe I've committed suicide!
Out of my body, I
look at myself and cry...
as my soul returns
with breathe of life,
I realize.....
All I have in this world is,

Me, Myself & I

Rocky Bradford

Intertwining Souls

ME

In quiet study trying to stay awake, I pray to myself I'm trying to have faith.

Random thoughts from life, death and my family

Sent to West Central wondering if she still loves me

If I hear anything different I might break free.

They're lucky they locked the door and threw away the key.

Each day I sink further and further into that abyss

Legs already in I am clinching the grass between my fists.

Trying to pull myself up towards the positive,

But my thoughts and depression sends me back into the negative.

All I can do is to leave it to something spiritual.

Praying for God to please grant me this miracle

Legs finally out with my knees touching the ground.

God heard my prayers go up and he sent blessings down.

As I stand to sit on my throne

With no more thoughts about the rights or the wrongs

I'm doing this for ME!!!

I'm doing this for ME...

Rocky Bradford

Intertwining Souls

The mind of Adam:

Well, I am alone with only the guy in the sky
The reason I'm here for, I have no clue why
All responsibility on me, all for me to decide
I can't do this alone, there's too much to do
wish someone else was here with me too
Why is it me to name all these animals?
All are tangible but so many to handle
Guess I have to find the light in my brain
Then forth ignite it like a candle
I have so much land to roam and to explore
But for some reason in the back of my mind
I want to know more, and what everything is for
Looks like I'm about to have an adventure in store.

Blake the snake

2/29/16

Intertwining Souls

My Lines

I was tiny, once of a seed,
Till mortal man and their contraptions
Condensing me into a smaller state again.
Infused with achromatic rock,
Orchestrated like a ballet,
Going along with the movements.
Piecing together a story,
Each precise stroke applied,
Having a meaning of some sort.
In which,
I'm unaware,
Fluent I'm not?
Till the beholder
Controlling the strings
Keeps on making me dance,
Understanding the skit,
Mastering the art,
Giving a performance.
Silenced and focused
I begin to skate along the parchment,
Till I'm finished.
Leaving nothing but a speck,
Signifying the end.
The audience in awing,
Waiting for the next chapter,
Instead blockage,
Unable to go further,
I move on,
Forcing myself to become duller and duller
To the point of snapping,

Intertwining Souls

I pause while..
Obtaining clarity to sharpen my senses,
Because I know the show must go on.
As I approached and my lips gently kiss the stage of what will become my canvas,
I prance along from left to right forming the plot.
Admirers from far bending out their chairs--
Astonished and amazed of witnessing something celestial,
Meanwhile,
Absorbing their inspired attention.
Thinking it's the powerful, mystic works of me!
Flattered I am, but instead,
I can not credit it,
I'm possessed by the eyes of the beholder.
THE PUPPET MASTER.
THE AUTHOR.
MY OWNER.

Rocky Bradford

Intertwining Souls

Remember

When I look at the stars at night..... I wonder if things are alright.... when I look at the moon above.... I remember my mom and her love....when I remember her face I can see her smile..... She is so far away, way more than miles..... I remember how happy she was.... how happy she made all of us.... I miss her more than I can say... I'll never forget that day... I remember that doctor saying that her life had come to an end.... I didn't believe it, it couldn't be true....she couldn't be taken from me and you.... I'll just remember my mom and her love....shell keep shining on us from up above.... when I look to the stars at night.... I wonder if everything's going to be alright... I'll remember she's there to guide us with her light...

Tiffany & Aubrey Willhelm

Intertwining Souls

SAYIN GOODBYE

I've never thought this would happen,
me saying good bye,
I thought what we had was special,
till you abandon my life,
Its too hard to say goodbye,
We've been thru many trials and tribulations,
the effort,
the sweat,
time and energy spent,
to come this far and just give up!
It's so hard to say goodbye,
just to let you go,
out my life and leave,
thought what we had was love,
instead, denial it was,
blinded by a substance,
an illusion of compassion and affection,
but I can't say good bye!!,
until both of us were free and able to see,
fighting to regain that spark,
you gave up and lost faith,
becoming the heartless one,
who left me!
I didn't want you to go,
now noticing,
you were holding me back,
my vision is clearer now,
without you by my side,
now that I've said it!
I'm glad I SAID GOODBYE!!! ~Rocky Bradford

Intertwining Souls

Slave 2 the Needle

Can anyone tell me why I am a slave 2 the needle???

Fighting between life and death and Heroin's in the middle

I've done everything in this world in order to get my fix

From robberies, thefts and trickin' out my ***ch

For what though?

To have the devils poison inside my rig!

Several hours pass to withdraws of the sneezes, chills and shits

My body keeps on feinin' man it's time for more licks

But in my head I really had enough I really wanna quit…

Yo, this dope isn't a drug it's a serious disease

Fighting thru this addiction so I dropped to my knees

Intertwining Souls

I sincerely asked God for salvation, pretty please???

Anticipating and waiting patiently

God whispers in my ear and said "He was the Key!"

I wake up not knowing if it was real or a dream

But I still wonder....

If I'm still a slave 2 this needle

As I come back to reality

I realize...

God has solved my riddle.

Rocky Bradford

Intertwining Souls

Solo Riches of Life

Solo riches of life

Passing thru the fingers of mortal man

Different outcomes to all

Except inevitable death

In which, we all shall experience

Therefore, aint trembled by fear

Unconsciously neither unsteady nor prepared

The taunting demons of old

Seeking retribution to all of those

Masked by sins of the apple

Patient shadows swarming

To the spirit

Feeding to emptiness

As its nothing more

Than just a coffin

Rocky Bradford

Intertwining Souls

SOMETIMES

For no real reason at all
My world goes dark
Everything beautiful fades away
And only endless black remains
There's no rhyme or reason
No particular event
No defining moment that sets it off
I just wake up one day
And my heart hurts
And my chest is heavy
And the most beautiful things
The things in life that are full of wonder and light
The things that should make me the happiest
Makes me want to weep
Makes me want to scream
Makes me hate the world
There's a wave of rage inside me
And the fact that I can't justify its presence
Only makes me angrier
When I look into my daughters beautiful hazel eyes
Eyes that are her mother's
I can see them pleading with me
Calling out for me to come back from the brink
Begging me not to jump
Those eyes have seen so much in her short 5 years
So much
And even though I know she can't see the darkness
I know she can sense its presence
And I want so bad to be better
For her

Intertwining Souls

For my son
Who already battles his own black plague

I want to be the hero that they so badly need
The hero that for the most part they believe I am
I want to be fearless and strong
I want to prevail
I want to banish these demons
That for so long have taken hostage the dark corners of my mind
But today all I can do is put my hand to the glass
And promise that I'll be back soon
And I will
The bad times don't last forever
But sometimes
For no reason at all
My world goes dark

Timi Dickason

Intertwining Souls

-shhh-

There's always this one question in my mind....
Why should a good woman be a secret all the time?
I know that I'm worth it, it these men that make me feel worthless!
Shhhh..... let's keep this on the hush,
Let's make sure this stays between us!

They say "KNOW UR WORTH!"
How can u do such a thing when all's u knows is hurt?
So I stay alone for many years, but at some point & time I want someone around to erase all my fears!
IT'S A LONELY WORLD BEING A NOBODY 2 SOMEBODY

Martrice White

The mind of Eve:

Took a bite off the apple that came from the tree of good and evil
The serpent tricked me, I have now damned all of the people
Made a mistake, now I'm walking on pins and needles
With the peak of curiosity, I became deceivable
Changed my fate, and all women forever
I made it worse rather than better
Causing women pain during birth and periods
How powerful one mistake can impact has me delirious

Blake the Snake

2/29/16

Intertwining Souls

The Snake

I have a quiet mouth but a loud mind
A snake with venom but does not bite
A fire within that is waiting to ignite
I contemplate about my thoughts at night
I keep them inside of my brain
I want to be positive so I hide the pain
Actions speak louder than words
I just wish that I could be somehow heard
Writing my thoughts is what works
By using metaphors and adverbs
I can heal where many people hurt
We were all put in the world for a reason
Make the world better then you leave it
Life is a game, can you defeat it?
Yes you can, if you believe it
your mind is what will help you achieve it.
Set your mind to all of your goals
and life will be a yellow brick road
Have a great day everyone, much love.

Blake the snake
March 7th, 2016

Intertwining Souls

THE TALK

GOD came to me in an apparition or so called vision,
he spoke to me with determination and wisely wisdom.
He told me about creating Adam &Eve in his likeness,
he said "believing in him that thy shall not parish."
We spoke long during our debate and conversation,
God said "Don't commit adultery unless thy is married."
He explained to me, how Moses parted the Red Sea.
God showed me how he made a blossoming flower from an ugly seed.
Overwhelmed with questions, I asked what you have in store for me.
Do I have a purpose in life, is that why you gave me the gift to breath?
Then I asked if I'll go to heaven for when I die?
God said "I would be tested by faith, only I could decide."
"That's why I gave you the power of free will, only you can make up your mind."
As the clouds closed together and we were saying our good-byes,
God finally said, " If we believe in him that it would lead us to that amazing, bright light.

Rocky Bradford

Intertwining Souls

UNTITLED

Sleepless night...
Mind wondering...
Heart hurting...
Is this it?
Or is there more?
Figuring out life's mysteries;
conjuring whatever stews up.
Chest filled in with cement,
As the pumping slowly comes to a stop.
I am speechless...
Wondering if they notice
But, they are blinded by their dark silk veal
Unaware of their actions
Still breathing as my world comes to a stop.
Should I say something?
Or still pretend I am okay?
Should I give a hint?
But they might miss it anyways.
So I'm still going to proceed on
as I wear my smile too
Cover up all my pain.

Rocky Bradford

Devour

I can't think about you.
The way you are when you're with me.
And when I'm not there.
You're someone else completely.

Its a tug of war you put me into.
A back and forth, like the rising sea.
I could not drift among the ocean.
Like Poseidon, you've devoured me.

Andrew Cornelius

Intertwining Souls

YOURSELF

Dark rays of laminating light

Bouncing off joyful smiles

Hiding the true colors

Of precious societies

Ones view of one another

Setting tones of separation

Creating boundaries

Preserving characters

But why?

Why do we hide from our true self's?

As if we are trembling in fear of others opinions

HA!!!

This is where our conscience gets in the way

The angel and devil starring you straight in the face

Telling you this and telling you that

Misleading you all together

Too the factual conclusion of life!

Live strong and prosper

And become an angel of your own belief

Disregarding the thoughts or views of others

Intertwining Souls

And see as far as you can see

And blossom and bloom in the best individual of all YOURSELF.

Rocky Bradford

Intertwining Souls

WE ARE

Victims...WE ALL HAVE BEEN OR KNOW OF ONE...

Kicked around, let down and turned away

That was no fun,

Then the clouds gave way to the sun one day....

With it a voice inside saying "WE ARE and a victim I will be no more, this is

DONE!!!"

Life is a game

but it's not fair

Even so I don't care

I was born with all this flare

required to remain the one ..no one can compare

But this night WE ARE

the ultimate STAR...

SUPERNOVA

Out and Ova!!!!!

Starla Mullins

Intertwining Souls

Still Me

I've battled evil
from the chains I broke free
I hold my head high, cause
I'm sweetly broken and still me

I'm no longer ashamed of my scars
they prove the fight I hold
I no longer feel hate
I'm no longer so cold

I'm simply misunderstood
I'm not a bad person u see
I've made my choices and yet
I'm sweetly broken and still me

My past doesn't define who I am
it no longer has that control
it tried to take over my heart
it tried to take over my soul

Some said I'd always remain the same
that perfection was the key
I just smiled and simply said
I'm sweetly broken and still me

Who is u to judge the life I live
was ur perfection seen
next time u want to point fingers
make sure ur hands are clean

I thank God every day
for reminding me who I'm meant to be
I'm no one perfect
I'm sweetly broken and still me

~Briana Smith

Intertwining Souls

HOW DO I LET U GO

I wrote this in rehab, it's to my ex that committed suicide in 2010, R. I. P. Seth.....

How do I say goodbye to u
how do I let u go
how do I gain closer
I need to know

Everything about u filled my heart
ur laugh, ur smile, ur eyes
our life gave me so much happiness
then I was left with nothing but cries

I remember the warmth of ur heart
the way we we're once in love
now the only way to talk to u
Is to ask the Lord above

U meant so much to me
oh how I miss u so
now I have to learn to move on
and how to let u go

What made u feel u cud no longer go on
why was death the way instead of life
we we're supposed to grow old together
u we're going to make me ur wife

I need to tell u I'm sorry
and I'll always love u so much
I wish I could take it all back
oh God how I missed ur touch

See I held all this grief and guilt
It kept so sad and so low
they say I need to be stronger
yet again, how do I let u go

Intertwining Souls

I stress for answers and knowledge
wonderin why u felt it was the answer
It tears me apart
eating at me like cancer

I guess I have to accept it
I guess I'll never know
yet I ask again
how do I let u go

I miss u more than u know
and I know ur looking down on me
ull always remain in my heart
from all this guilt, I need to be free

Until the day we meet again
In my heart ull remain forever so
now I have to move on
I have to let u go!

Briana Smith

Intertwining Souls

"I Am"

I am a survivor and a fighter
I wonder if that's obvious to see
I hear all the voices telling me
I see what u can be
I want to scream to them all
I am a survivor and a fighter

I pretend to be stronger than I am
I feel my scars leaking tears
I touch, yet I feel nothing
I worry u can see my fears
I cry for my losses, but I stop and remember
I am a survivor and a fighter

I understand I can't change the past
I say u can't undo what's been done
I dream that it's all a game
I try to believe I won
I hope everyone can see
I am a survivor and a fighter

Briana Smith

Intertwining Souls

Cant Cope

I'm slowly drowning with a smile on my face.

But you cannot see behind the mask of the tears falling down on to my cheeks.

You can't see how much my heart is tearing itself apart at the thought of you being gone.

You see my stone face when you think I'm hurting.

You can't see what hell in facing and hear the demons laughter.

They know what they're doing and I can't stop them.

If only I could scream out loud for your hand or just your help.

But you are no longer there and so I fall deep down in this hole.

Only to be surrounded by the darkness that I've fought so hard to beat.

The pain I buried has been slowly clawing it's way out of the grave to haunt me.

Just please, when you leave, take my heart with you so I don't have to feel this again.

Alec Toy

Intertwining Souls

Not Forever Tho

To the love of my life and keeper of this heart I've housed
though fate never allowed me to make you my spouse...
When we met over two years ago
it was love at first sight that I know.
I loved you so much and for only you I cared
but with you those feelings I never shared.
Then I learned for another you cared.
To come between you I never dared.
Not because I did not want to
but because I wanted happiness for you.
Then to the arms of another I did go
but with him, love I never did know.
For this I now know that I was wrong
for all these years your love I've longed.
Of you I have thought throughout the years.
For you I have shed so many tears.
So long ago I solemnly vowed
to tell of my love if fate allowed.
Our paths crossed again not so long ago.
I remembered the vow of my love you should know.
Before I could tell you, you gave a surprise.
You told me you loved me and brought tears to my eyes.
You told of your love and how much you cared
how you felt sad that this you had not shared.
You said that you felt you had told me too late
and for this you said you I must hate.
But it is you I love and never could hate
To know of your love is never too late.
You told me of things you wanted to do
all of this and more I have wanted too.
All this time I have dreamed of your touch
to know you wanted the same means so much.
We have shared so much from the present and past.
I have prayed so much that this would last.

Intertwining Souls

You have told me that what we want is wrong
how can this be when we have loved so long?
Something happened and we fell apart
crushing my dreams and breaking my heart.
To love you was a gift from above.
The gift of time, the gift of love.
My heart won't allow me to let you go,
it wants and misses you so.
I tried to leave to mend the pain,
but it's about to drive me insane.
Saddened and hurting my heart goes on
knowing again that you are gone.
Because in your hands is where my heart lies
alone and depressed it sadly cries.
Please know that this is how I truly feel
because twice in my life you have made it all real.
I know you had feelings that you just would not show.
I know that it hurts when you want to let go.
My actions say yes but heart still says no.
I will never get to feel your most intimate touch.
God knows though I love and miss you so much.
I love you with my heart and soul.
You made me feel loved, you made me feel whole.
I have always known that you are the one for me.
I still believe though you say it can't be.
There is one thing that I have to say
I love you too much to just walk away.
We said goodbye but I want you to know.
Goodbye is goodbye but not forever though

~Starla Mullins

Intertwining Souls
This Pisces

Resourceful is he who comes from pain

Years of repetition always being the same

yet to internalize all and to reflect none

Made this Pisces fall, like Icarus from sun

Heavy hearted fiend from just before

Dwells on regret until brain becomes sore

So many years discarded without care

Necessity of needle more precious than air

Never to know of what comes next

Not working the muscle, it's pointless to flex

Return my body so this mind may follow

Fulfillment awaits this decline from hollow

An infatuation that took so very much

Walking through life as if on a crutch

not falling at all, rising as of late

Changing life's direction breeds a new fate

CraigMicheal~

Intertwining Souls

Dream of Despair

As I step into the darkness I feel total despair. No recollection of time or why im standing there. I feel an intense fear pulsing through my veins. It seems more frigid than normal and it starts to rain. Bloodcurdling screams sound so Satanic. You don't know what is happening so you panic. A satanic situation in this heavy precipitation. Trying to have a conversation because I demand an explanation. I see a figure approaching from the distance. "Confront it or hide?" Is what im thinking at this instance? My heart is pounding out of my chest, is this some kind of exam or test? Walking up is a little boy in his Sunday best, his eyes filled with conquest. His voice is so powerful and chilling to the bone. Worst part about this is I know we're not alone. He places his palm upon my shoulder I become colder and colder. I stare into his eyes as they begin to smolder. He says "my child this might hurt a little bit, please don't scream." Im manic, I panic, my mind is running frantic. I close my eyes and open them it was jus a dream.

Alan W. Roberts II

Intertwining Souls

I hope you enjoyed these poems from these individuals that were willing to share their experiences along with mine. Here is a special sneak peek to my next book I am writing.

Intertwining Souls

Gospel of Elon: The First Born Death

Lilith, Adams first wife, is banished from heaven and upon this banishment takes her first stab at God by taking the life of her first victim baby, Elon. In Heaven the children that have died of unfortunate events still gets the pleasure to age up to the age of 18.

Elon's a few days away from his birthday and God requests his presence. God asks Elon if he would like to live on earth as a gift for he is coming to his age and is willing to give Elon a second chance at life. Secretively, God feels guilty that the banishment of Lilith caused his death.

The question is Elon has lived in Heaven for 18yrs and has never sinned; Elon's been pure and has only read texts of sin. How is Elon going to live on a place that's full of it? Are the sins of mortal men going to corrupt Elon's holiness and break the channel between him and Heaven? Or by the help of the prophet Ishmael on earth could prevent him from such corruption. But how hard is it going to be? Especially once he sets his eyes upon the dazzling Victoria Armstrong.

Does Elon sin and loses his chance to return to Heaven? Or do the teachings of the prophet Ishmael help Elon from breaking the channel and dimming his halo...

To be continued...

Intertwining Souls

Made in the USA
Middletown, DE
10 May 2018